Bills And Payments Organizer

This book belongs to:

....

....

IF FOUND CONTACT:

....

• Contents •

• Bonus Chapters •

• SUBSCRIPTIONS TRACKER •

SUBSCRIPTION	DUE ON	AMOUNT	FREQUENCY		AUTO RENEW	
			Monthly	Yearly	Yes	No
1.		$	○	○	○	○
2.		$	○	○	○	○
3.		$	○	○	○	○
4.		$	○	○	○	○
5.		$	○	○	○	○
6.		$	○	○	○	○
7.		$	○	○	○	○
8.		$	○	○	○	○
9.		$	○	○	○	○
10.		$	○	○	○	○
11.		$	○	○	○	○
12.		$	○	○	○	○
13.		$	○	○	○	○
14.		$	○	○	○	○
15.		$	○	○	○	○
16.		$	○	○	○	○
17.		$	○	○	○	○
18.		$	○	○	○	○
19.		$	○	○	○	○
20.		$	○	○	○	○
21.		$	○	○	○	○

• SUBSCRIPTIONS TRACKER •

SUBSCRIPTION	DUE ON	AMOUNT	FREQUENCY		AUTO RENEW	
			Monthly	Yearly	Yes	No
22.		$	○	○	○	○
23.		$	○	○	○	○
24.		$	○	○	○	○
25.		$	○	○	○	○
26.		$	○	○	○	○
27.		$	○	○	○	○
28.		$	○	○	○	○
29.		$	○	○	○	○
30.		$	○	○	○	○
31.		$	○	○	○	○
32.		$	○	○	○	○
33.		$	○	○	○	○
34.		$	○	○	○	○
35.		$	○	○	○	○
36.		$	○	○	○	○
37.		$	○	○	○	○
38.		$	○	○	○	○
39.		$	○	○	○	○
40.		$	○	○	○	○
41.		$	○	○	○	○
42.		$	○	○	○	○

• SUBSCRIPTIONS TRACKER •

SUBSCRIPTION	DUE ON	AMOUNT	FREQUENCY		AUTO RENEW	
			Monthly	Yearly	Yes	No
43.		$	◯	◯	◯	◯
44.		$	◯	◯	◯	◯
45.		$	◯	◯	◯	◯
46.		$	◯	◯	◯	◯
47.		$	◯	◯	◯	◯
48.		$	◯	◯	◯	◯
49.		$	◯	◯	◯	◯
50.		$	◯	◯	◯	◯
51.		$	◯	◯	◯	◯
52.		$	◯	◯	◯	◯
53.		$	◯	◯	◯	◯
54.		$	◯	◯	◯	◯
55.		$	◯	◯	◯	◯
56.		$	◯	◯	◯	◯
57.		$	◯	◯	◯	◯
58.		$	◯	◯	◯	◯
59.		$	◯	◯	◯	◯
60.		$	◯	◯	◯	◯
61.		$	◯	◯	◯	◯
62.		$	◯	◯	◯	◯
63.		$	◯	◯	◯	◯

Bills & Payments

**ORGANIZE, PLAN AND TRACK
MONTHLY BILLS, EXPENSES & PAYMENTS**

MONTHLY BILLS CALENDAR

YEAR:

JAN FEB MAR APR MAY JUN JUL AUG SEPT OCT NOV DEC

SUN	MON	TUE	WED	THU	FRI	SAT

Notes

• BILL PAYMENTS •

BILL TO BE PAID	DATE DUE	AMOUNT DUE	AMOUNT PAID	PAID	*Notes*
		$	$	○	
		$	$	○	
		$	$	○	
		$	$	○	
		$	$	○	
		$	$	○	
		$	$	○	
		$	$	○	
		$	$	○	
		$	$	○	
		$	$	○	
		$	$	○	
		$	$	○	
		$	$	○	
		$	$	○	
		$	$	○	
		$	$	○	
		$	$	○	
		$	$	○	
		$	$	○	
	TOTAL	$	$		

MONTHLY BILLS CALENDAR

YEAR:

JAN FEB MAR APR MAY JUN JUL AUG SEPT OCT NOV DEC

SUN	MON	TUE	WED	THU	FRI	SAT

Notes

• BILL PAYMENTS •

BILL TO BE PAID	DATE DUE	AMOUNT DUE	AMOUNT PAID	PAID	Notes
		$	$	○	
		$	$	○	
		$	$	○	
		$	$	○	
		$	$	○	
		$	$	○	
		$	$	○	
		$	$	○	
		$	$	○	
		$	$	○	
		$	$	○	
		$	$	○	
		$	$	○	
		$	$	○	
		$	$	○	
		$	$	○	
		$	$	○	
		$	$	○	
		$	$	○	
		$	$	○	
	TOTAL	$	$		

MONTHLY BILLS CALENDAR

YEAR:

JAN FEB MAR APR MAY JUN JUL AUG SEPT OCT NOV DEC

SUN	MON	TUE	WED	THU	FRI	SAT

Notes

• BILL PAYMENTS •

BILL TO BE PAID	DATE DUE	AMOUNT DUE	AMOUNT PAID	PAID	Notes
		$	$	○	
		$	$	○	
		$	$	○	
		$	$	○	
		$	$	○	
		$	$	○	
		$	$	○	
		$	$	○	
		$	$	○	
		$	$	○	
		$	$	○	
		$	$	○	
		$	$	○	
		$	$	○	
		$	$	○	
		$	$	○	
		$	$	○	
		$	$	○	
		$	$	○	
		$	$	○	
	TOTAL	$	$		

MONTHLY BILLS CALENDAR

YEAR:

JAN FEB MAR APR MAY JUN JUL AUG SEPT OCT NOV DEC

SUN	MON	TUE	WED	THU	FRI	SAT

Notes

• BILL PAYMENTS •

BILL TO BE PAID	DATE DUE	AMOUNT DUE	AMOUNT PAID	PAID	Notes
		$	$	◯	
		$	$	◯	
		$	$	◯	
		$	$	◯	
		$	$	◯	
		$	$	◯	
		$	$	◯	
		$	$	◯	
		$	$	◯	
		$	$	◯	
		$	$	◯	
		$	$	◯	
		$	$	◯	
		$	$	◯	
		$	$	◯	
		$	$	◯	
		$	$	◯	
		$	$	◯	
		$	$	◯	
		$	$	◯	
	TOTAL	$	$		

MONTHLY BILLS CALENDAR

YEAR:

JAN FEB MAR APR MAY JUN JUL AUG SEPT OCT NOV DEC

SUN	MON	TUE	WED	THU	FRI	SAT

Notes

• BILL PAYMENTS •

BILL TO BE PAID	DATE DUE	AMOUNT DUE	AMOUNT PAID	PAID	Notes
		$	$		
		$	$		
		$	$		
		$	$		
		$	$		
		$	$		
		$	$		
		$	$		
		$	$		
		$	$		
		$	$		
		$	$		
		$	$		
		$	$		
		$	$		
		$	$		
		$	$		
		$	$		
		$	$		
		$	$		
	TOTAL	$	$		

MONTHLY BILLS CALENDAR

YEAR:

JAN FEB MAR APR MAY JUN JUL AUG SEPT OCT NOV DEC

SUN	MON	TUE	WED	THU	FRI	SAT

Notes

• BILL PAYMENTS •

BILL TO BE PAID	DATE DUE	AMOUNT DUE	AMOUNT PAID	PAID	*Notes*
		$	$	○	
		$	$	○	
		$	$	○	
		$	$	○	
		$	$	○	
		$	$	○	
		$	$	○	
		$	$	○	
		$	$	○	
		$	$	○	
		$	$	○	
		$	$	○	
		$	$	○	
		$	$	○	
		$	$	○	
		$	$	○	
		$	$	○	
		$	$	○	
		$	$	○	
		$	$	○	
	TOTAL	$	$		

MONTHLY BILLS CALENDAR

YEAR:

JAN FEB MAR APR MAY JUN JUL AUG SEPT OCT NOV DEC

SUN	MON	TUE	WED	THU	FRI	SAT

Notes

• BILL PAYMENTS •

BILL TO BE PAID	DATE DUE	AMOUNT DUE	AMOUNT PAID	PAID	Notes
		$	$	○	
		$	$	○	
		$	$	○	
		$	$	○	
		$	$	○	
		$	$	○	
		$	$	○	
		$	$	○	
		$	$	○	
		$	$	○	
		$	$	○	
		$	$	○	
		$	$	○	
		$	$	○	
		$	$	○	
		$	$	○	
		$	$	○	
		$	$	○	
		$	$	○	
		$	$	○	
TOTAL		$	$		

MONTHLY BILLS CALENDAR

YEAR:

JAN FEB MAR APR MAY JUN JUL AUG SEPT OCT NOV DEC

SUN	MON	TUE	WED	THU	FRI	SAT

Notes

• BILL PAYMENTS •

BILL TO BE PAID	DATE DUE	AMOUNT DUE	AMOUNT PAID	PAID	Notes
		$	$	○	
		$	$	○	
		$	$	○	
		$	$	○	
		$	$	○	
		$	$	○	
		$	$	○	
		$	$	○	
		$	$	○	
		$	$	○	
		$	$	○	
		$	$	○	
		$	$	○	
		$	$	○	
		$	$	○	
		$	$	○	
		$	$	○	
		$	$	○	
		$	$	○	
		$	$	○	
TOTAL		$	$		

MONTHLY BILLS CALENDAR

YEAR:

JAN FEB MAR APR MAY JUN JUL AUG SEPT OCT NOV DEC

SUN	MON	TUE	WED	THU	FRI	SAT

Notes

• BILL PAYMENTS •

BILL TO BE PAID	DATE DUE	AMOUNT DUE	AMOUNT PAID	PAID	Notes
		$	$	○	
		$	$	○	
		$	$	○	
		$	$	○	
		$	$	○	
		$	$	○	
		$	$	○	
		$	$	○	
		$	$	○	
		$	$	○	
		$	$	○	
		$	$	○	
		$	$	○	
		$	$	○	
		$	$	○	
		$	$	○	
		$	$	○	
		$	$	○	
		$	$	○	
		$	$	○	
TOTAL		$	$		

MONTHLY BILLS CALENDAR

YEAR:

JAN FEB MAR APR MAY JUN JUL AUG SEPT OCT NOV DEC

SUN	MON	TUE	WED	THU	FRI	SAT

Notes

• BILL PAYMENTS •

BILL TO BE PAID	DATE DUE	AMOUNT DUE	AMOUNT PAID	PAID	*Notes*
		$	$	○	
		$	$	○	
		$	$	○	
		$	$	○	
		$	$	○	
		$	$	○	
		$	$	○	
		$	$	○	
		$	$	○	
		$	$	○	
		$	$	○	
		$	$	○	
		$	$	○	
		$	$	○	
		$	$	○	
		$	$	○	
		$	$	○	
		$	$	○	
		$	$	○	
		$	$	○	
TOTAL		$	$		

MONTHLY BILLS CALENDAR

YEAR:

JAN FEB MAR APR MAY JUN JUL AUG SEPT OCT NOV DEC

SUN	MON	TUE	WED	THU	FRI	SAT

Notes

• BILL PAYMENTS •

BILL TO BE PAID	DATE DUE	AMOUNT DUE	AMOUNT PAID	PAID	Notes
		$	$	○	
		$	$	○	
		$	$	○	
		$	$	○	
		$	$	○	
		$	$	○	
		$	$	○	
		$	$	○	
		$	$	○	
		$	$	○	
		$	$	○	
		$	$	○	
		$	$	○	
		$	$	○	
		$	$	○	
		$	$	○	
		$	$	○	
		$	$	○	
		$	$	○	
		$	$	○	
	TOTAL	$	$		

MONTHLY BILLS CALENDAR

YEAR:

JAN FEB MAR APR MAY JUN JUL AUG SEPT OCT NOV DEC

SUN	MON	TUE	WED	THU	FRI	SAT

Notes

• BILL PAYMENTS •

BILL TO BE PAID	DATE DUE	AMOUNT DUE	AMOUNT PAID	PAID	Notes
		$	$	○	
		$	$	○	
		$	$	○	
		$	$	○	
		$	$	○	
		$	$	○	
		$	$	○	
		$	$	○	
		$	$	○	
		$	$	○	
		$	$	○	
		$	$	○	
		$	$	○	
		$	$	○	
		$	$	○	
		$	$	○	
		$	$	○	
		$	$	○	
		$	$	○	
		$	$	○	
TOTAL		$	$		

MONTHLY BILLS CALENDAR

YEAR:

JAN FEB MAR APR MAY JUN JUL AUG SEPT OCT NOV DEC

SUN	MON	TUE	WED	THU	FRI	SAT

Notes

• BILL PAYMENTS •

BILL TO BE PAID	DATE DUE	AMOUNT DUE	AMOUNT PAID	PAID	Notes
		$	$	◯	
		$	$	◯	
		$	$	◯	
		$	$	◯	
		$	$	◯	
		$	$	◯	
		$	$	◯	
		$	$	◯	
		$	$	◯	
		$	$	◯	
		$	$	◯	
		$	$	◯	
		$	$	◯	
		$	$	◯	
		$	$	◯	
		$	$	◯	
		$	$	◯	
		$	$	◯	
		$	$	◯	
		$	$	◯	
	TOTAL	$	$		

MONTHLY BILLS CALENDAR

YEAR:

JAN FEB MAR APR MAY JUN JUL AUG SEPT OCT NOV DEC

SUN	MON	TUE	WED	THU	FRI	SAT

Notes

• BILL PAYMENTS •

BILL TO BE PAID	DATE DUE	AMOUNT DUE	AMOUNT PAID	PAID	Notes
		$	$	◯	
		$	$	◯	
		$	$	◯	
		$	$	◯	
		$	$	◯	
		$	$	◯	
		$	$	◯	
		$	$	◯	
		$	$	◯	
		$	$	◯	
		$	$	◯	
		$	$	◯	
		$	$	◯	
		$	$	◯	
		$	$	◯	
		$	$	◯	
		$	$	◯	
		$	$	◯	
		$	$	◯	
		$	$	◯	
	TOTAL	$	$		

MONTHLY BILLS CALENDAR

YEAR:

JAN FEB MAR APR MAY JUN JUL AUG SEPT OCT NOV DEC

SUN	MON	TUE	WED	THU	FRI	SAT

Notes

• BILL PAYMENTS •

BILL TO BE PAID	DATE DUE	AMOUNT DUE	AMOUNT PAID	PAID	Notes
		$	$	◯	
		$	$	◯	
		$	$	◯	
		$	$	◯	
		$	$	◯	
		$	$	◯	
		$	$	◯	
		$	$	◯	
		$	$	◯	
		$	$	◯	
		$	$	◯	
		$	$	◯	
		$	$	◯	
		$	$	◯	
		$	$	◯	
		$	$	◯	
		$	$	◯	
		$	$	◯	
		$	$	◯	
		$	$	◯	
	TOTAL	$	$		

MONTHLY BILLS CALENDAR

YEAR:

JAN FEB MAR APR MAY JUN JUL AUG SEPT OCT NOV DEC

SUN	MON	TUE	WED	THU	FRI	SAT

Notes

• BILL PAYMENTS •

BILL TO BE PAID	DATE DUE	AMOUNT DUE	AMOUNT PAID	PAID	Notes
		$	$	◯	
		$	$	◯	
		$	$	◯	
		$	$	◯	
		$	$	◯	
		$	$	◯	
		$	$	◯	
		$	$	◯	
		$	$	◯	
		$	$	◯	
		$	$	◯	
		$	$	◯	
		$	$	◯	
		$	$	◯	
		$	$	◯	
		$	$	◯	
		$	$	◯	
		$	$	◯	
		$	$	◯	
		$	$	◯	
	TOTAL	$	$		

MONTHLY BILLS CALENDAR

YEAR:

JAN FEB MAR APR MAY JUN JUL AUG SEPT OCT NOV DEC

SUN	MON	TUE	WED	THU	FRI	SAT

Notes

• BILL PAYMENTS •

BILL TO BE PAID	DATE DUE	AMOUNT DUE	AMOUNT PAID	PAID	Notes
		$	$	◯	
		$	$	◯	
		$	$	◯	
		$	$	◯	
		$	$	◯	
		$	$	◯	
		$	$	◯	
		$	$	◯	
		$	$	◯	
		$	$	◯	
		$	$	◯	
		$	$	◯	
		$	$	◯	
		$	$	◯	
		$	$	◯	
		$	$	◯	
		$	$	◯	
		$	$	◯	
		$	$	◯	
		$	$	◯	
	TOTAL	$	$		

MONTHLY BILLS CALENDAR

YEAR:

JAN FEB MAR APR MAY JUN JUL AUG SEPT OCT NOV DEC

SUN	MON	TUE	WED	THU	FRI	SAT

Notes

• BILL PAYMENTS •

BILL TO BE PAID	DATE DUE	AMOUNT DUE	AMOUNT PAID	PAID	Notes
		$	$	○	
		$	$	○	
		$	$	○	
		$	$	○	
		$	$	○	
		$	$	○	
		$	$	○	
		$	$	○	
		$	$	○	
		$	$	○	
		$	$	○	
		$	$	○	
		$	$	○	
		$	$	○	
		$	$	○	
		$	$	○	
		$	$	○	
		$	$	○	
		$	$	○	
		$	$	○	
	TOTAL	$	$		

MONTHLY BILLS CALENDAR

YEAR:

JAN FEB MAR APR MAY JUN JUL AUG SEPT OCT NOV DEC

SUN	MON	TUE	WED	THU	FRI	SAT

Notes

• BILL PAYMENTS •

BILL TO BE PAID	DATE DUE	AMOUNT DUE	AMOUNT PAID	PAID	Notes
		$	$	◯	
		$	$	◯	
		$	$	◯	
		$	$	◯	
		$	$	◯	
		$	$	◯	
		$	$	◯	
		$	$	◯	
		$	$	◯	
		$	$	◯	
		$	$	◯	
		$	$	◯	
		$	$	◯	
		$	$	◯	
		$	$	◯	
		$	$	◯	
		$	$	◯	
		$	$	◯	
		$	$	◯	
		$	$	◯	
	TOTAL	$	$		

MONTHLY BILLS CALENDAR

YEAR:

JAN FEB MAR APR MAY JUN JUL AUG SEPT OCT NOV DEC

SUN	MON	TUE	WED	THU	FRI	SAT

Notes

• BILL PAYMENTS •

BILL TO BE PAID	DATE DUE	AMOUNT DUE	AMOUNT PAID	PAID	*Notes*
		$	$	○	
		$	$	○	
		$	$	○	
		$	$	○	
		$	$	○	
		$	$	○	
		$	$	○	
		$	$	○	
		$	$	○	
		$	$	○	
		$	$	○	
		$	$	○	
		$	$	○	
		$	$	○	
		$	$	○	
		$	$	○	
		$	$	○	
		$	$	○	
		$	$	○	
		$	$	○	
	TOTAL	$	$		

MONTHLY BILLS CALENDAR

YEAR:

JAN FEB MAR APR MAY JUN JUL AUG SEPT OCT NOV DEC

SUN	MON	TUE	WED	THU	FRI	SAT

Notes

• BILL PAYMENTS •

BILL TO BE PAID	DATE DUE	AMOUNT DUE	AMOUNT PAID	PAID	*Notes*
		$	$	◯	
		$	$	◯	
		$	$	◯	
		$	$	◯	
		$	$	◯	
		$	$	◯	
		$	$	◯	
		$	$	◯	
		$	$	◯	
		$	$	◯	
		$	$	◯	
		$	$	◯	
		$	$	◯	
		$	$	◯	
		$	$	◯	
		$	$	◯	
		$	$	◯	
		$	$	◯	
		$	$	◯	
		$	$	◯	
	TOTAL	$	$		

MONTHLY BILLS CALENDAR

YEAR:

JAN FEB MAR APR MAY JUN JUL AUG SEPT OCT NOV DEC

SUN	MON	TUE	WED	THU	FRI	SAT

Notes

• BILL PAYMENTS •

BILL TO BE PAID	DATE DUE	AMOUNT DUE	AMOUNT PAID	PAID	Notes
		$	$	○	
		$	$	○	
		$	$	○	
		$	$	○	
		$	$	○	
		$	$	○	
		$	$	○	
		$	$	○	
		$	$	○	
		$	$	○	
		$	$	○	
		$	$	○	
		$	$	○	
		$	$	○	
		$	$	○	
		$	$	○	
		$	$	○	
		$	$	○	
		$	$	○	
		$	$	○	
TOTAL		$	$		

MONTHLY BILLS CALENDAR

YEAR:

JAN FEB MAR APR MAY JUN JUL AUG SEPT OCT NOV DEC

SUN	MON	TUE	WED	THU	FRI	SAT

Notes

• BILL PAYMENTS •

BILL TO BE PAID	DATE DUE	AMOUNT DUE	AMOUNT PAID	PAID	*Notes*
		$	$	○	
		$	$	○	
		$	$	○	
		$	$	○	
		$	$	○	
		$	$	○	
		$	$	○	
		$	$	○	
		$	$	○	
		$	$	○	
		$	$	○	
		$	$	○	
		$	$	○	
		$	$	○	
		$	$	○	
		$	$	○	
		$	$	○	
		$	$	○	
		$	$	○	
		$	$	○	
	TOTAL	$	$		

MONTHLY BILLS CALENDAR

YEAR:

JAN FEB MAR APR MAY JUN JUL AUG SEPT OCT NOV DEC

SUN	MON	TUE	WED	THU	FRI	SAT

Notes

• BILL PAYMENTS •

BILL TO BE PAID	DATE DUE	AMOUNT DUE	AMOUNT PAID	PAID	Notes
		$	$	○	
		$	$	○	
		$	$	○	
		$	$	○	
		$	$	○	
		$	$	○	
		$	$	○	
		$	$	○	
		$	$	○	
		$	$	○	
		$	$	○	
		$	$	○	
		$	$	○	
		$	$	○	
		$	$	○	
		$	$	○	
		$	$	○	
		$	$	○	
		$	$	○	
		$	$	○	
	TOTAL	$	$		

MONTHLY BILLS CALENDAR

YEAR:

JAN FEB MAR APR MAY JUN JUL AUG SEPT OCT NOV DEC

SUN	MON	TUE	WED	THU	FRI	SAT

Notes

• BILL PAYMENTS •

BILL TO BE PAID	DATE DUE	AMOUNT DUE	AMOUNT PAID	PAID	Notes
		$	$	◯	
		$	$	◯	
		$	$	◯	
		$	$	◯	
		$	$	◯	
		$	$	◯	
		$	$	◯	
		$	$	◯	
		$	$	◯	
		$	$	◯	
		$	$	◯	
		$	$	◯	
		$	$	◯	
		$	$	◯	
		$	$	◯	
		$	$	◯	
		$	$	◯	
		$	$	◯	
		$	$	◯	
		$	$	◯	
	TOTAL	$	$		

MONTHLY BILLS CALENDAR

YEAR:

JAN FEB MAR APR MAY JUN JUL AUG SEPT OCT NOV DEC

SUN	MON	TUE	WED	THU	FRI	SAT

Notes

• BILL PAYMENTS •

BILL TO BE PAID	DATE DUE	AMOUNT DUE	AMOUNT PAID	PAID	*Notes*
		$	$	◯	
		$	$	◯	
		$	$	◯	
		$	$	◯	
		$	$	◯	
		$	$	◯	
		$	$	◯	
		$	$	◯	
		$	$	◯	
		$	$	◯	
		$	$	◯	
		$	$	◯	
		$	$	◯	
		$	$	◯	
		$	$	◯	
		$	$	◯	
		$	$	◯	
		$	$	◯	
		$	$	◯	
		$	$	◯	
TOTAL		$	$		

MONTHLY BILLS CALENDAR

YEAR:

JAN FEB MAR APR MAY JUN JUL AUG SEPT OCT NOV DEC

SUN	MON	TUE	WED	THU	FRI	SAT

Notes

• BILL PAYMENTS •

BILL TO BE PAID	DATE DUE	AMOUNT DUE	AMOUNT PAID	PAID	Notes
		$	$	○	
		$	$	○	
		$	$	○	
		$	$	○	
		$	$	○	
		$	$	○	
		$	$	○	
		$	$	○	
		$	$	○	
		$	$	○	
		$	$	○	
		$	$	○	
		$	$	○	
		$	$	○	
		$	$	○	
		$	$	○	
		$	$	○	
		$	$	○	
		$	$	○	
		$	$	○	
	TOTAL	$	$		

MONTHLY BILLS CALENDAR

YEAR:

JAN FEB MAR APR MAY JUN JUL AUG SEPT OCT NOV DEC

SUN	MON	TUE	WED	THU	FRI	SAT

Notes

• BILL PAYMENTS •

BILL TO BE PAID	DATE DUE	AMOUNT DUE	AMOUNT PAID	PAID	Notes
		$	$	○	
		$	$	○	
		$	$	○	
		$	$	○	
		$	$	○	
		$	$	○	
		$	$	○	
		$	$	○	
		$	$	○	
		$	$	○	
		$	$	○	
		$	$	○	
		$	$	○	
		$	$	○	
		$	$	○	
		$	$	○	
		$	$	○	
		$	$	○	
		$	$	○	
		$	$	○	
	TOTAL	$	$		

MONTHLY BILLS CALENDAR

YEAR:

JAN FEB MAR APR MAY JUN JUL AUG SEPT OCT NOV DEC

SUN	MON	TUE	WED	THU	FRI	SAT

Notes

• BILL PAYMENTS •

BILL TO BE PAID	DATE DUE	AMOUNT DUE	AMOUNT PAID	PAID	Notes
		$	$	○	
		$	$	○	
		$	$	○	
		$	$	○	
		$	$	○	
		$	$	○	
		$	$	○	
		$	$	○	
		$	$	○	
		$	$	○	
		$	$	○	
		$	$	○	
		$	$	○	
		$	$	○	
		$	$	○	
		$	$	○	
		$	$	○	
		$	$	○	
		$	$	○	
		$	$	○	
	TOTAL	$	$		

MONTHLY BILLS CALENDAR

YEAR:

JAN FEB MAR APR MAY JUN JUL AUG SEPT OCT NOV DEC

SUN	MON	TUE	WED	THU	FRI	SAT

Notes

• BILL PAYMENTS •

BILL TO BE PAID	DATE DUE	AMOUNT DUE	AMOUNT PAID	PAID	Notes
		$	$	◯	
		$	$	◯	
		$	$	◯	
		$	$	◯	
		$	$	◯	
		$	$	◯	
		$	$	◯	
		$	$	◯	
		$	$	◯	
		$	$	◯	
		$	$	◯	
		$	$	◯	
		$	$	◯	
		$	$	◯	
		$	$	◯	
		$	$	◯	
		$	$	◯	
		$	$	◯	
		$	$	◯	
		$	$	◯	
	TOTAL	$	$		

MONTHLY BILLS CALENDAR

YEAR:

JAN FEB MAR APR MAY JUN JUL AUG SEPT OCT NOV DEC

SUN	MON	TUE	WED	THU	FRI	SAT

Notes

• BILL PAYMENTS •

BILL TO BE PAID	DATE DUE	AMOUNT DUE	AMOUNT PAID	PAID	Notes
		$	$	○	
		$	$	○	
		$	$	○	
		$	$	○	
		$	$	○	
		$	$	○	
		$	$	○	
		$	$	○	
		$	$	○	
		$	$	○	
		$	$	○	
		$	$	○	
		$	$	○	
		$	$	○	
		$	$	○	
		$	$	○	
		$	$	○	
		$	$	○	
		$	$	○	
		$	$	○	
TOTAL		$	$		

MONTHLY BILLS CALENDAR

YEAR:

JAN FEB MAR APR MAY JUN JUL AUG SEPT OCT NOV DEC

SUN	MON	TUE	WED	THU	FRI	SAT

Notes

• BILL PAYMENTS •

BILL TO BE PAID	DATE DUE	AMOUNT DUE	AMOUNT PAID	PAID	Notes
		$	$	○	
		$	$	○	
		$	$	○	
		$	$	○	
		$	$	○	
		$	$	○	
		$	$	○	
		$	$	○	
		$	$	○	
		$	$	○	
		$	$	○	
		$	$	○	
		$	$	○	
		$	$	○	
		$	$	○	
		$	$	○	
		$	$	○	
		$	$	○	
		$	$	○	
		$	$	○	
TOTAL		$	$		

MONTHLY BILLS CALENDAR

YEAR:

JAN FEB MAR APR MAY JUN JUL AUG SEPT OCT NOV DEC

SUN	MON	TUE	WED	THU	FRI	SAT

Notes

• BILL PAYMENTS •

BILL TO BE PAID	DATE DUE	AMOUNT DUE	AMOUNT PAID	PAID	Notes
		$	$	○	
		$	$	○	
		$	$	○	
		$	$	○	
		$	$	○	
		$	$	○	
		$	$	○	
		$	$	○	
		$	$	○	
		$	$	○	
		$	$	○	
		$	$	○	
		$	$	○	
		$	$	○	
		$	$	○	
		$	$	○	
		$	$	○	
		$	$	○	
		$	$	○	
		$	$	○	
	TOTAL	$	$		

MONTHLY BILLS CALENDAR

YEAR:

JAN FEB MAR APR MAY JUN JUL AUG SEPT OCT NOV DEC

SUN	MON	TUE	WED	THU	FRI	SAT

Notes

• BILL PAYMENTS •

BILL TO BE PAID	DATE DUE	AMOUNT DUE	AMOUNT PAID	PAID	*Notes*
		$	$	○	
		$	$	○	
		$	$	○	
		$	$	○	
		$	$	○	
		$	$	○	
		$	$	○	
		$	$	○	
		$	$	○	
		$	$	○	
		$	$	○	
		$	$	○	
		$	$	○	
		$	$	○	
		$	$	○	
		$	$	○	
		$	$	○	
		$	$	○	
		$	$	○	
		$	$	○	
TOTAL		$	$		

MONTHLY BILLS CALENDAR

YEAR:

JAN FEB MAR APR MAY JUN JUL AUG SEPT OCT NOV DEC

SUN	MON	TUE	WED	THU	FRI	SAT

Notes

• BILL PAYMENTS •

BILL TO BE PAID	DATE DUE	AMOUNT DUE	AMOUNT PAID	PAID	Notes
		$	$	○	
		$	$	○	
		$	$	○	
		$	$	○	
		$	$	○	
		$	$	○	
		$	$	○	
		$	$	○	
		$	$	○	
		$	$	○	
		$	$	○	
		$	$	○	
		$	$	○	
		$	$	○	
		$	$	○	
		$	$	○	
		$	$	○	
		$	$	○	
		$	$	○	
		$	$	○	
	TOTAL	$	$		

MONTHLY BILLS CALENDAR

YEAR:

JAN FEB MAR APR MAY JUN JUL AUG SEPT OCT NOV DEC

SUN	MON	TUE	WED	THU	FRI	SAT

Notes

• BILL PAYMENTS •

BILL TO BE PAID	DATE DUE	AMOUNT DUE	AMOUNT PAID	PAID	Notes
		$	$	○	
		$	$	○	
		$	$	○	
		$	$	○	
		$	$	○	
		$	$	○	
		$	$	○	
		$	$	○	
		$	$	○	
		$	$	○	
		$	$	○	
		$	$	○	
		$	$	○	
		$	$	○	
		$	$	○	
		$	$	○	
		$	$	○	
		$	$	○	
		$	$	○	
		$	$	○	
	TOTAL	$	$		

Debt Pay-Off Tracker

**ORGANIZE, PLAN, AND TRACK
YOUR DEBT-FREE FUTURE**

• HOW TO USE THE DEBT-PAYOFF WORKSHEETS •

One of the more popular methods for paying off debt is known as the snowball method. This approach involves paying off your debts in order of smallest to largest, which can help you build momentum and motivation as you work toward becoming debt-free.

This section's worksheets are designed to assist you in applying this method. Or simply use them to track your balance if you follow any other strategies.

1. Use the **Payoff Priority Planner worksheet** to list all your debts from smallest to largest balance.

2. **Tackle your smallest debt first.**

   Pay as much as possible on the smallest debt (minimum due + extra) to pay it off as soon as you can.

   Minimum Due $ + Extra $ = New Payment $$ To Smallest Debt

   Continue to make minimum payments on all other debts.

3. Once the smallest debt is paid-off, roll that payment (minimum + extras) onto the next smallest debt on the list.

   Minimum Payment + Rollover = New Payment

4. Repeat until you are debt free!

PAY-OFF PRIORITY PLANNER

DEBT	BALANCE	MINIMUM PAYMENT	+	ROLLOVER	=	NEW PAYMENT	PAID OFF?
	$	$	+	$	=	$	
	$	$	+	$	=	$	
	$	$	+	$	=	$	
	$	$	+	$	=	$	
	$	$	+	$	=	$	
	$	$	+	$	=	$	
	$	$	+	$	=	$	
	$	$	+	$	=	$	
	$	$	+	$	=	$	
	$	$	+	$	=	$	
	$	$	+	$	=	$	
	$	$	+	$	=	$	
	$	$	+	$	=	$	
	$	$	+	$	=	$	
TOTAL	$	$					

PAY-OFF PRIORITY PLANNER

DEBT	BALANCE	MINIMUM PAYMENT	+	ROLLOVER	=	NEW PAYMENT	PAID OFF?
	$	$	+	$	=	$	○
	$	$	+	$	=	$	○
	$	$	+	$	=	$	○
	$	$	+	$	=	$	○
	$	$	+	$	=	$	○
	$	$	+	$	=	$	○
	$	$	+	$	=	$	○
	$	$	+	$	=	$	○
	$	$	+	$	=	$	○
	$	$	+	$	=	$	○
	$	$	+	$	=	$	○
	$	$	+	$	=	$	○
	$	$	+	$	=	$	○
	$	$	+	$	=	$	○
TOTAL	$	$					

Debt Pay-off Tracker

DEBT	CREDITOR
INTEREST RATE %	TERM
STARTING BALANCE $	PAYOFF DATE GOAL
MONTHLY PAYMENT MINIMUM $	MONTHLY PAYMENT GOAL $

• VISUAL TRACKER •

$ 100%

95%

$ 90%

85%

$ 80%

75%

$ 70%

65%

$ 60%

55%

$ 50%

45%

$ 40%

35%

$ 30%

25%

$ 20%

15%

$ 10%

5%

Color in the rows as you pay-off debt balance.

Notes

Debt Pay-off Tracker

DATE	PAYMENT	BALANCE	DATE	PAYMENT	BALANCE
	$	$		$	$
	$	$		$	$
	$	$		$	$
	$	$		$	$
	$	$		$	$
	$	$		$	$
	$	$		$	$
	$	$		$	$
	$	$		$	$
	$	$		$	$
	$	$		$	$
	$	$		$	$
	$	$		$	$
	$	$		$	$
	$	$		$	$
	$	$		$	$

Debt Pay-off Tracker

DEBT	CREDITOR
INTEREST RATE %	TERM
STARTING BALANCE $	PAYOFF DATE GOAL
MONTHLY PAYMENT MINIMUM $	MONTHLY PAYMENT GOAL $

• VISUAL TRACKER •

$		100%
	95%	
$		90%
	85%	
$		80%
	75%	
$		70%
	65%	
$		60%
	55%	
$		50%
	45%	
$		40%
	35%	
$		30%
	25%	
$		20%
	15%	
$		10%
	5%	

Color in the rows as you pay-off debt balance.

Notes

Debt Pay-off Tracker

DATE	PAYMENT	BALANCE	DATE	PAYMENT	BALANCE
	$	$		$	$
	$	$		$	$
	$	$		$	$
	$	$		$	$
	$	$		$	$
	$	$		$	$
	$	$		$	$
	$	$		$	$
	$	$		$	$
	$	$		$	$
	$	$		$	$
	$	$		$	$
	$	$		$	$
	$	$		$	$
	$	$		$	$
	$	$		$	$

DEBT PAY-OFF TRACKER

DEBT	CREDITOR
INTEREST RATE %	TERM
STARTING BALANCE $	PAYOFF DATE GOAL
MONTHLY PAYMENT MINIMUM $	MONTHLY PAYMENT GOAL $

• VISUAL TRACKER •

$ 100%

95%

$ 90%

85%

$ 80%

75%

$ 70%

65%

$ 60%

55%

$ 50%

45%

$ 40%

35%

$ 30%

25%

$ 20%

15%

$ 10%

5%

Color in the rows as you pay-off debt balance.

Notes

Debt Pay-off Tracker

DATE	PAYMENT	BALANCE
	$	$
	$	$
	$	$
	$	$
	$	$
	$	$
	$	$
	$	$
	$	$
	$	$
	$	$
	$	$
	$	$
	$	$
	$	$
	$	$

DATE	PAYMENT	BALANCE
	$	$
	$	$
	$	$
	$	$
	$	$
	$	$
	$	$
	$	$
	$	$
	$	$
	$	$
	$	$
	$	$
	$	$
	$	$
	$	$

Debt Pay-off Tracker

DEBT	CREDITOR
INTEREST RATE %	TERM
STARTING BALANCE $	PAYOFF DATE GOAL
MONTHLY PAYMENT MINIMUM $	MONTHLY PAYMENT GOAL $

• VISUAL TRACKER •

$ 100%

95%

$ 90%

85%

$ 80%

75%

$ 70%

65%

$ 60%

55%

$ 50%

45%

$ 40%

35%

$ 30%

25%

$ 20%

15%

$ 10%

5%

Color in the rows as you pay-off debt balance.

Notes

Debt Pay-off Tracker

DATE	PAYMENT	BALANCE	DATE	PAYMENT	BALANCE
	$	$		$	$
	$	$		$	$
	$	$		$	$
	$	$		$	$
	$	$		$	$
	$	$		$	$
	$	$		$	$
	$	$		$	$
	$	$		$	$
	$	$		$	$
	$	$		$	$
	$	$		$	$
	$	$		$	$
	$	$		$	$
	$	$		$	$
	$	$		$	$

DEBT PAY-OFF TRACKER

DEBT	CREDITOR
INTEREST RATE %	TERM
STARTING BALANCE $	PAYOFF DATE GOAL
MONTHLY PAYMENT MINIMUM $	MONTHLY PAYMENT GOAL $

• VISUAL TRACKER •

$ 100%

95%

$ 90%

85%

$ 80%

75%

$ 70%

65%

$ 60%

55%

$ 50%

45%

$ 40%

35%

$ 30%

25%

$ 20%

15%

$ 10%

5%

Color in the rows as you pay-off debt balance.

Notes

Debt Pay-off Tracker

DATE	PAYMENT	BALANCE	DATE	PAYMENT	BALANCE
	$	$		$	$
	$	$		$	$
	$	$		$	$
	$	$		$	$
	$	$		$	$
	$	$		$	$
	$	$		$	$
	$	$		$	$
	$	$		$	$
	$	$		$	$
	$	$		$	$
	$	$		$	$
	$	$		$	$
	$	$		$	$
	$	$		$	$
	$	$		$	$

DEBT PAY-OFF TRACKER

DEBT	CREDITOR
INTEREST RATE %	TERM
STARTING BALANCE $	PAYOFF DATE GOAL
MONTHLY PAYMENT MINIMUM $	MONTHLY PAYMENT GOAL $

• VISUAL TRACKER •

$ 100%

95%

$ 90%

85%

$ 80%

75%

$ 70%

65%

$ 60%

55%

$ 50%

45%

$ 40%

35%

$ 30%

25%

$ 20%

15%

$ 10%

5%

Color in the rows as you pay-off debt balance.

Notes

Debt Pay-off Tracker

DATE	PAYMENT	BALANCE
	$	$
	$	$
	$	$
	$	$
	$	$
	$	$
	$	$
	$	$
	$	$
	$	$
	$	$
	$	$
	$	$
	$	$
	$	$
	$	$

DATE	PAYMENT	BALANCE
	$	$
	$	$
	$	$
	$	$
	$	$
	$	$
	$	$
	$	$
	$	$
	$	$
	$	$
	$	$
	$	$
	$	$
	$	$
	$	$

DEBT PAY-OFF TRACKER

DEBT	CREDITOR
INTEREST RATE %	TERM
STARTING BALANCE $	PAYOFF DATE GOAL
MONTHLY PAYMENT MINIMUM $	MONTHLY PAYMENT GOAL $

• VISUAL TRACKER •

$ 100%

95%

$ 90%

85%

$ 80%

75%

$ 70%

65%

$ 60%

55%

$ 50%

45%

$ 40%

35%

$ 30%

25%

$ 20%

15%

$ 10%

5%

Color in the rows as you pay-off debt balance.

Notes

Debt Pay-off Tracker

DATE	PAYMENT	BALANCE
	$	$
	$	$
	$	$
	$	$
	$	$
	$	$
	$	$
	$	$
	$	$
	$	$
	$	$
	$	$
	$	$
	$	$
	$	$
	$	$

DATE	PAYMENT	BALANCE
	$	$
	$	$
	$	$
	$	$
	$	$
	$	$
	$	$
	$	$
	$	$
	$	$
	$	$
	$	$
	$	$
	$	$
	$	$
	$	$

Debt Pay-off Tracker

DEBT	CREDITOR
INTEREST RATE %	TERM
STARTING BALANCE $	PAYOFF DATE GOAL
MONTHLY PAYMENT MINIMUM $	MONTHLY PAYMENT GOAL $

• VISUAL TRACKER •

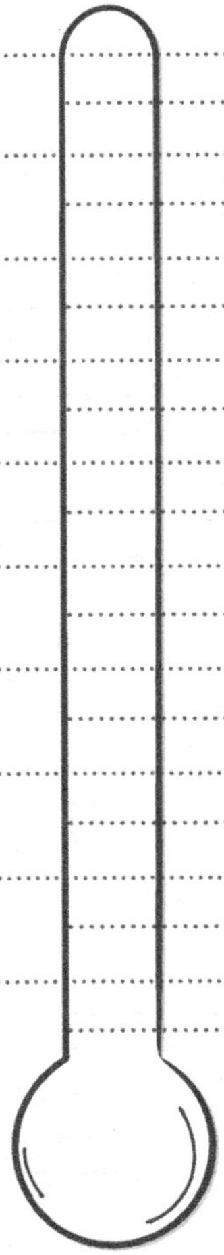

$		100%
	95%	
$		90%
	85%	
$		80%
	75%	
$		70%
	65%	
$		60%
	55%	
$		50%
	45%	
$		40%
	35%	
$		30%
	25%	
$		20%
	15%	
$		10%
	5%	

Color in the rows as you pay-off debt balance.

Notes

Debt Pay-off Tracker

DATE	PAYMENT	BALANCE	DATE	PAYMENT	BALANCE
	$	$		$	$
	$	$		$	$
	$	$		$	$
	$	$		$	$
	$	$		$	$
	$	$		$	$
	$	$		$	$
	$	$		$	$
	$	$		$	$
	$	$		$	$
	$	$		$	$
	$	$		$	$
	$	$		$	$
	$	$		$	$
	$	$		$	$
	$	$		$	$

Debt Pay-off Tracker

DEBT	CREDITOR
INTEREST RATE %	TERM
STARTING BALANCE $	PAYOFF DATE GOAL
MONTHLY PAYMENT MINIMUM $	MONTHLY PAYMENT GOAL $

• VISUAL TRACKER •

$		100%
	95%	
$		90%
	85%	
$		80%
	75%	
$		70%
	65%	
$		60%
	55%	
$		50%
	45%	
$		40%
	35%	
$		30%
	25%	
$		20%
	15%	
$		10%
	5%	

Color in the rows as you pay-off debt balance.

Notes

Debt Pay-off Tracker

DATE	PAYMENT	BALANCE
	$	$
	$	$
	$	$
	$	$
	$	$
	$	$
	$	$
	$	$
	$	$
	$	$
	$	$
	$	$
	$	$
	$	$
	$	$
	$	$

DATE	PAYMENT	BALANCE
	$	$
	$	$
	$	$
	$	$
	$	$
	$	$
	$	$
	$	$
	$	$
	$	$
	$	$
	$	$
	$	$
	$	$
	$	$
	$	$

Notes

Savings

PLAN AND MONITOR THE PROGRESS OF YOUR SAVINGS GOALS

Emergency Fund

• SAVINGS TRACKER •

Build an emergency fund to cover 6 months of expenses.

How to use this tracker- Each jar represents one month of expenses.
Each row represents ten percent of one month's expense.
Color in the rows as you save.

Savings Goal			Value of Each Row		
$ ______ (Monthly Expenses)	X 6 =	$ ______ (Savings Goal)	$ ______ (Monthly Expenses)	÷ 10 =	$ ______ (Value of Each Row)

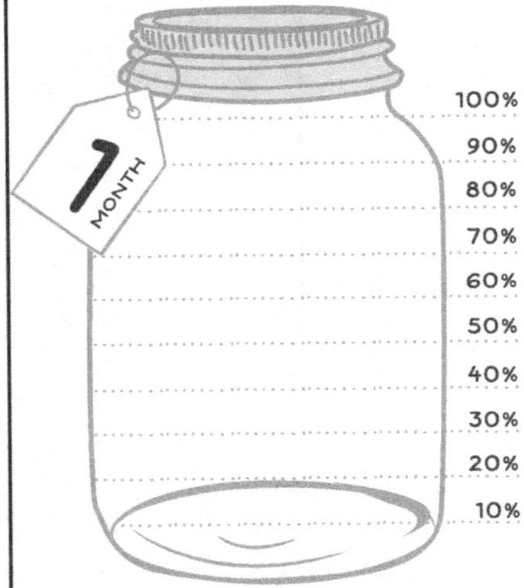

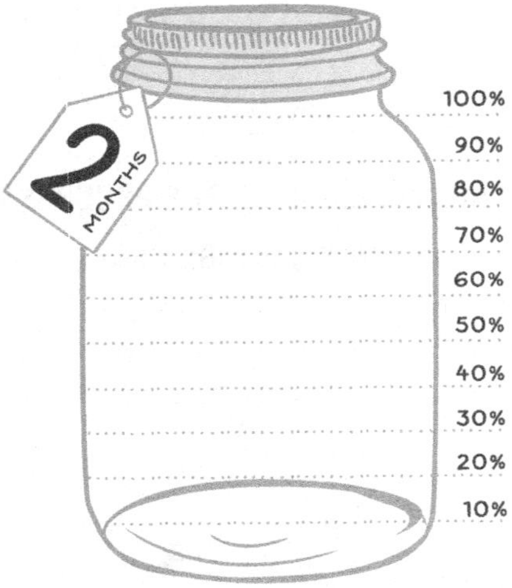

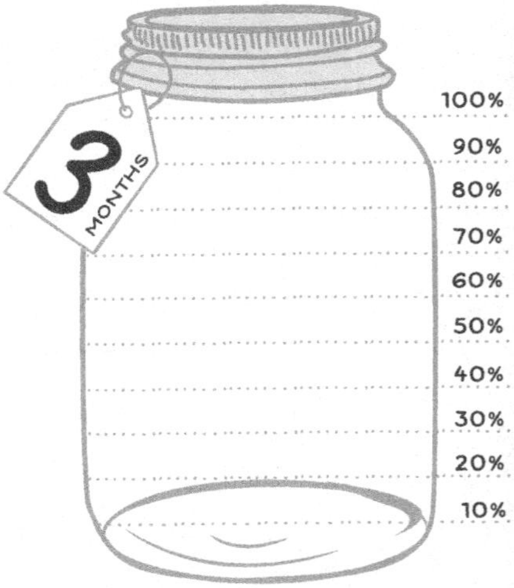

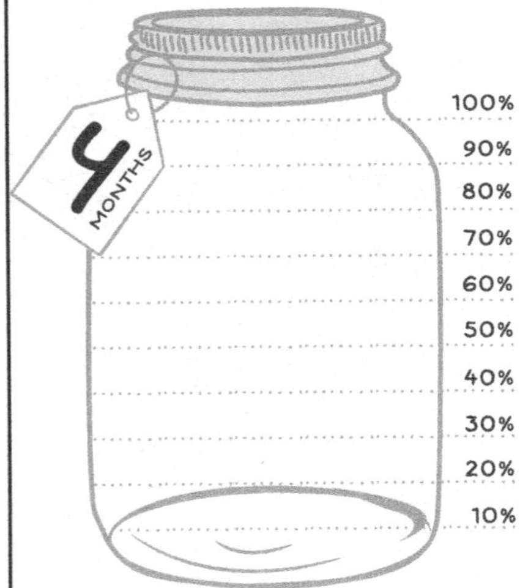

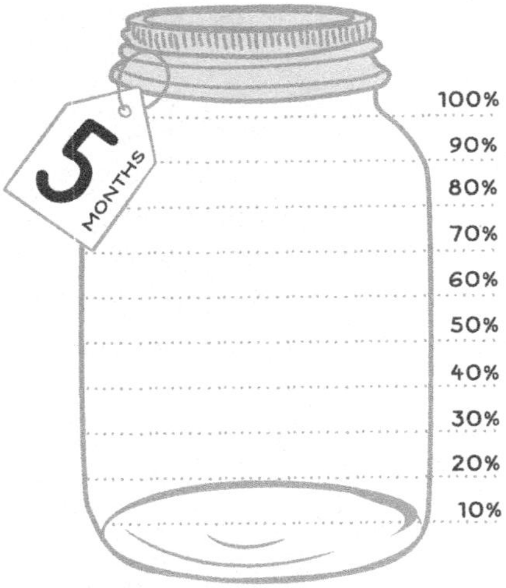

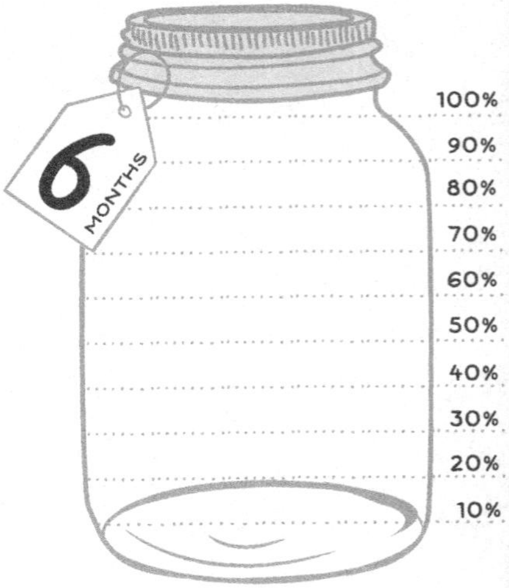

• SAVINGS TRACKER •

Emergency Fund

SAVINGS GOAL: $ ______________________

Date	Deposit	Date	Deposit
	$		$
	$		$
	$		$
	$		$
	$		$
	$		$
	$		$
	$		$
	$		$
	$		$
	$		$
	$		$
	$		$
	$		$
TOTAL SAVED	$	TOTAL SAVED	$

• SAVINGS TRACKER •

Fund For: ______________________________

SAVINGS GOAL: $ ______________________

Date	Deposit
	$
	$
	$
	$
	$
	$
	$
	$
	$
	$
	$
	$
	$

TOTAL SAVED: $

Notes:

____

____

____

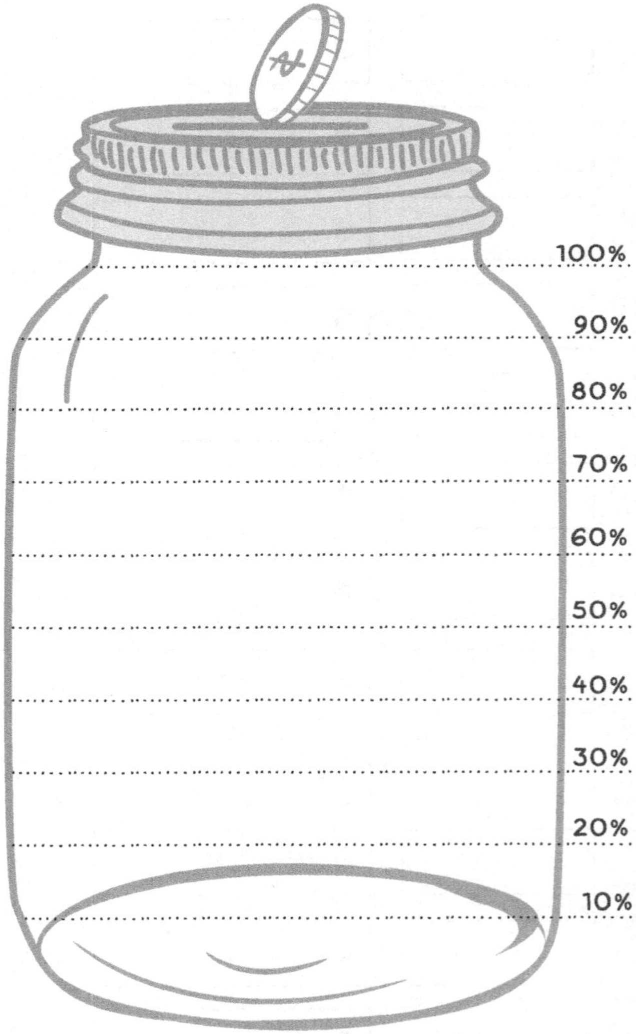

Color in the rows as you save.

• SAVINGS TRACKER •

Fund For: ______________________________

SAVINGS GOAL: $ ______________________

Date	Deposit
	$
	$
	$
	$
	$
	$
	$
	$
	$
	$
	$
	$
	$

TOTAL SAVED: $

Notes:

____

____

____

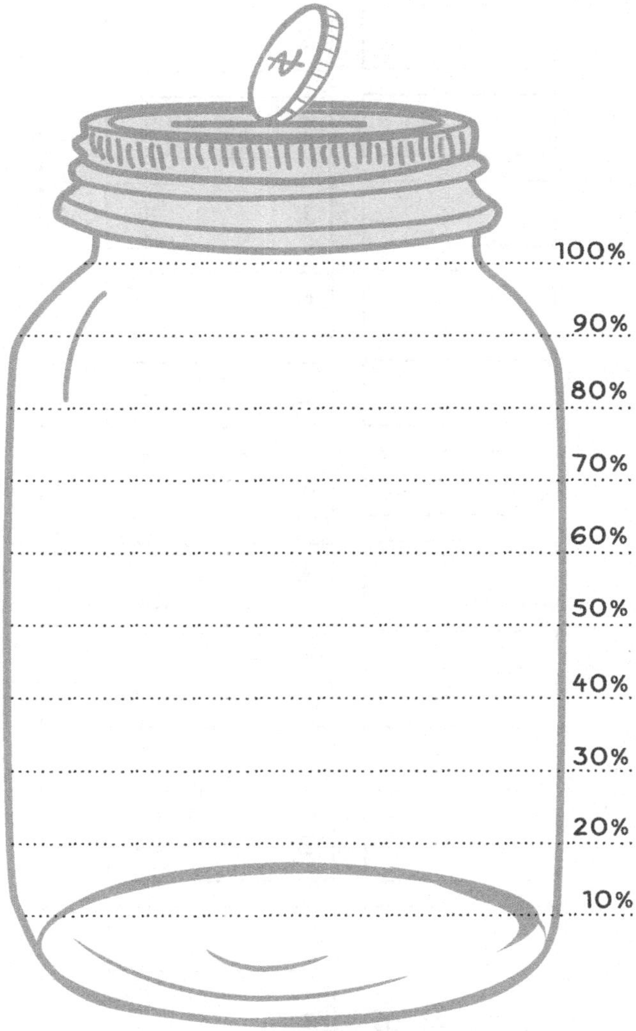

Color in the rows as you save.

• SAVINGS TRACKER •

Fund For: ______________________________

SAVINGS GOAL: $ ______________________

Date	Deposit
	$
	$
	$
	$
	$
	$
	$
	$
	$
	$
	$
	$
	$
TOTAL SAVED:	$

Notes: ______________________________

____

____

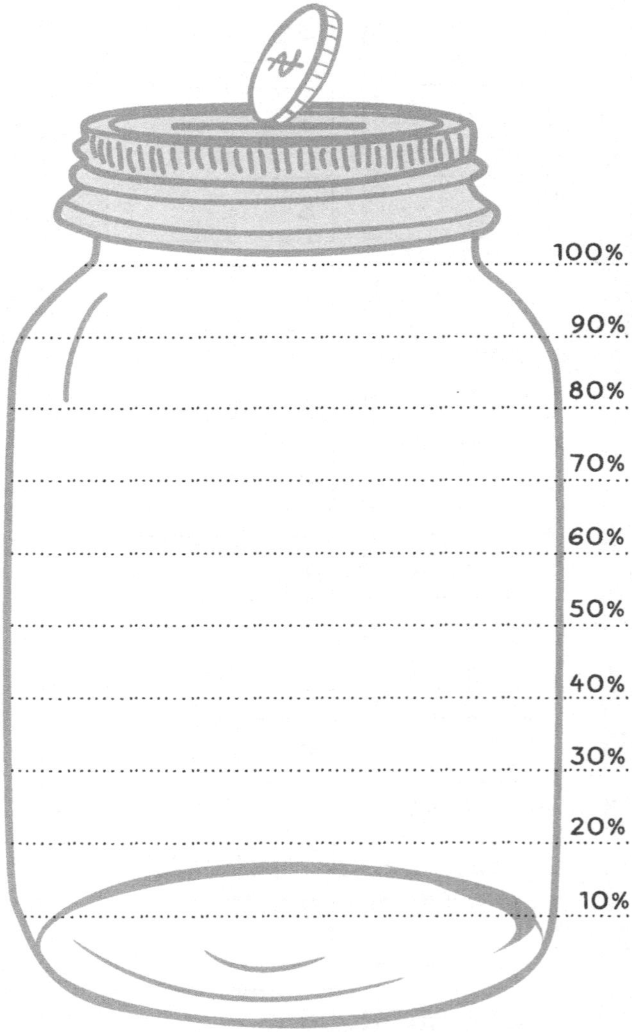

Color in the rows as you save.

• SAVINGS TRACKER •

Fund For: ______________________________

SAVINGS GOAL: $ ______________________

Date	Deposit
	$
	$
	$
	$
	$
	$
	$
	$
	$
	$
	$
	$
	$

TOTAL SAVED: $

Notes:

____

____

____

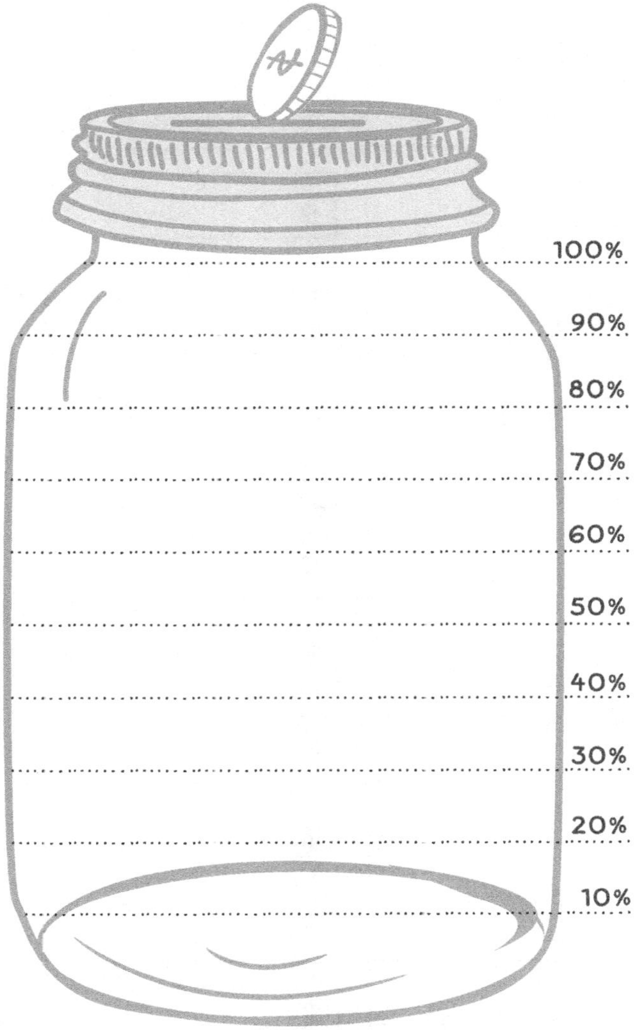

Color in the rows as you save.

• SAVINGS TRACKER •

Fund For: ______________________________

SAVINGS GOAL: $ ______________________

Date	Deposit
	$
	$
	$
	$
	$
	$
	$
	$
	$
	$
	$
	$
	$
TOTAL SAVED:	$

Notes: ______________________________

____

____

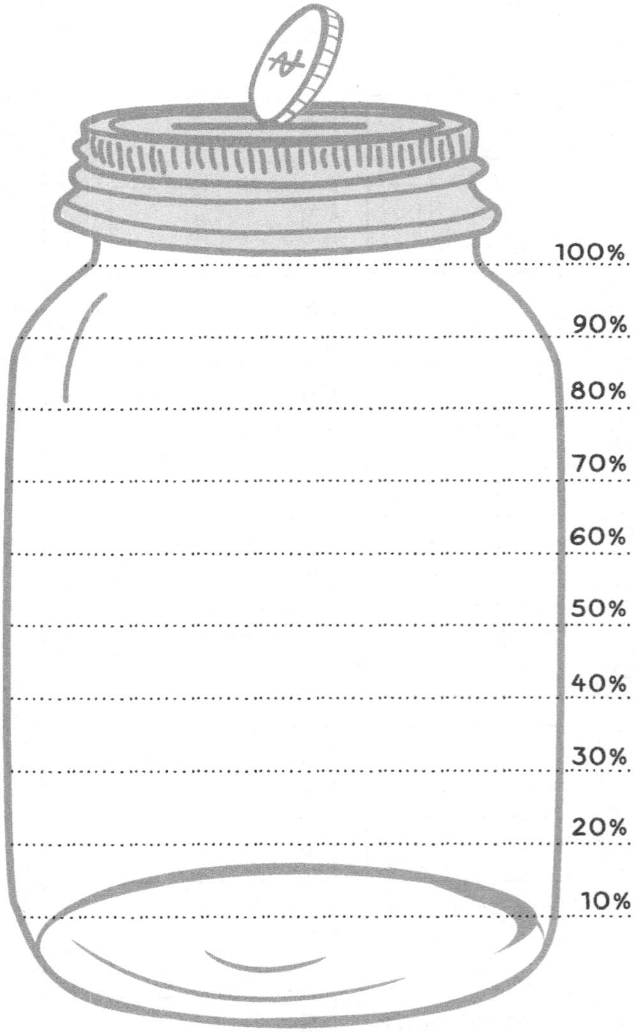

Color in the rows as you save.

• SAVINGS TRACKER •

Fund For: ______________________

SAVINGS GOAL: $ ______________________

Date	Deposit
	$
	$
	$
	$
	$
	$
	$
	$
	$
	$
	$
	$
	$
TOTAL SAVED:	$

Notes:

____

____

____

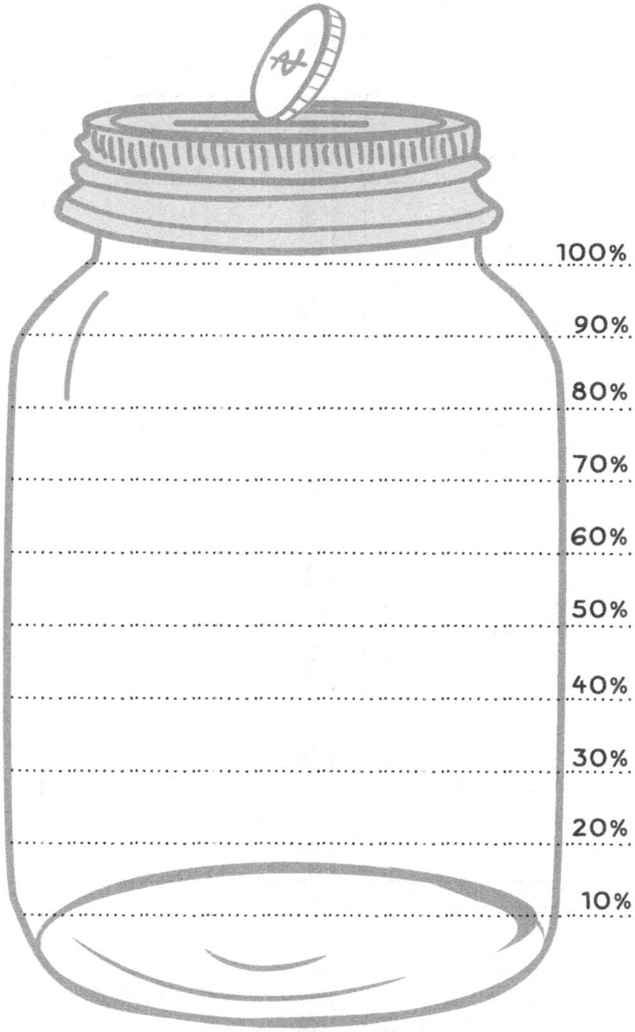

Color in the rows as you save.

• SAVINGS TRACKER •

Fund For: ______________________________

SAVINGS GOAL: $ ______________________

Date	Deposit
	$
	$
	$
	$
	$
	$
	$
	$
	$
	$
	$
	$
	$
TOTAL SAVED:	$

Notes:

____

____

____

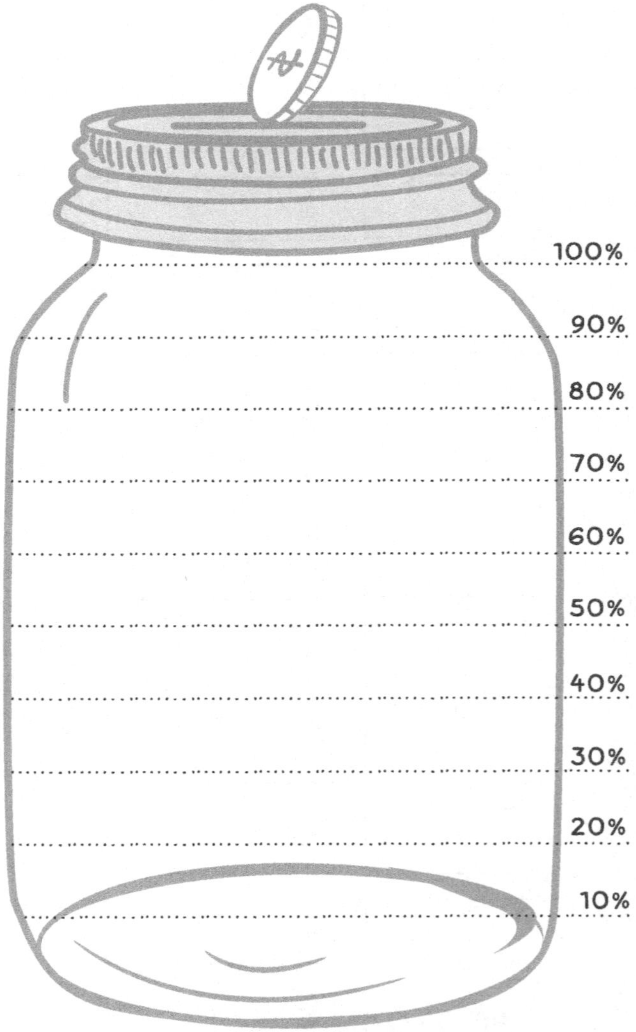

Color in the rows as you save.

• SAVINGS TRACKER •

Fund For: ____________________

SAVINGS GOAL: $ ____________________

Date	Deposit
	$
	$
	$
	$
	$
	$
	$
	$
	$
	$
	$
	$
	$
TOTAL SAVED:	$

Notes: ____________________

____

____

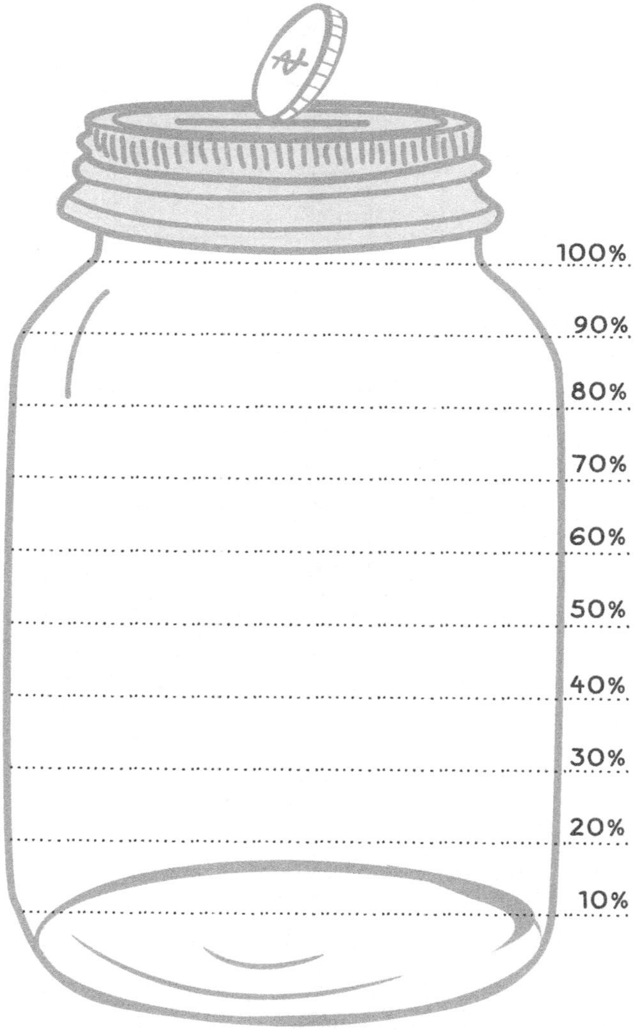

Color in the rows as you save.

• SAVINGS TRACKER •

Fund For: ______________________________

SAVINGS GOAL: $ ______________________

Date	Deposit
	$
	$
	$
	$
	$
	$
	$
	$
	$
	$
	$
	$
	$
TOTAL SAVED:	$

Notes: ______________________________

____

____

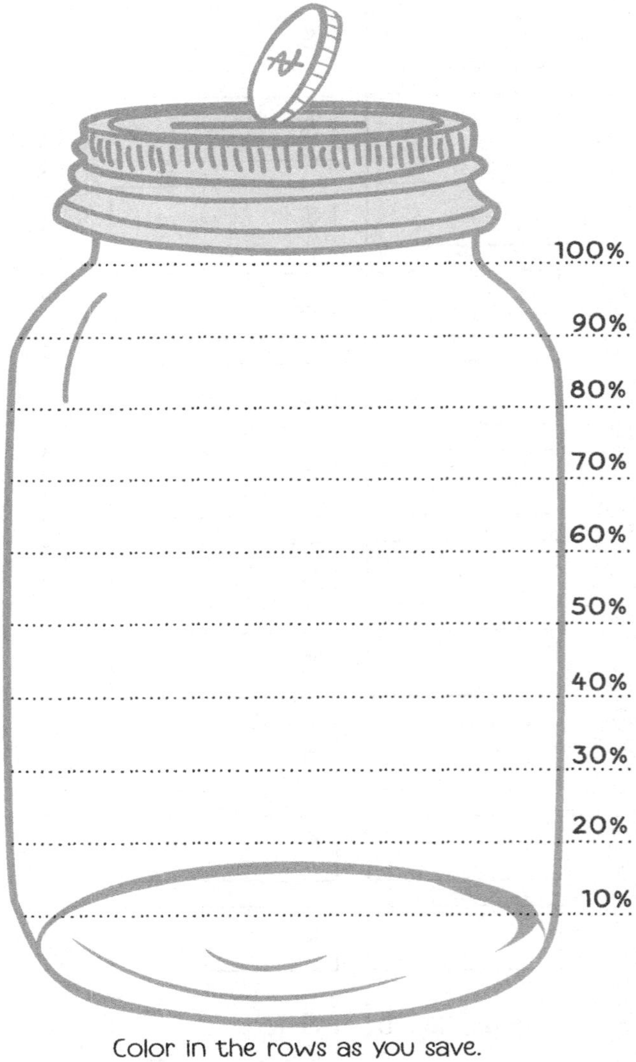

Color in the rows as you save.

• SAVINGS TRACKER •

Fund For: ______________________________

SAVINGS GOAL: $ ______________________________

Date	Deposit
	$
	$
	$
	$
	$
	$
	$
	$
	$
	$
	$
	$
	$

TOTAL SAVED: $

Notes:

____

____

____

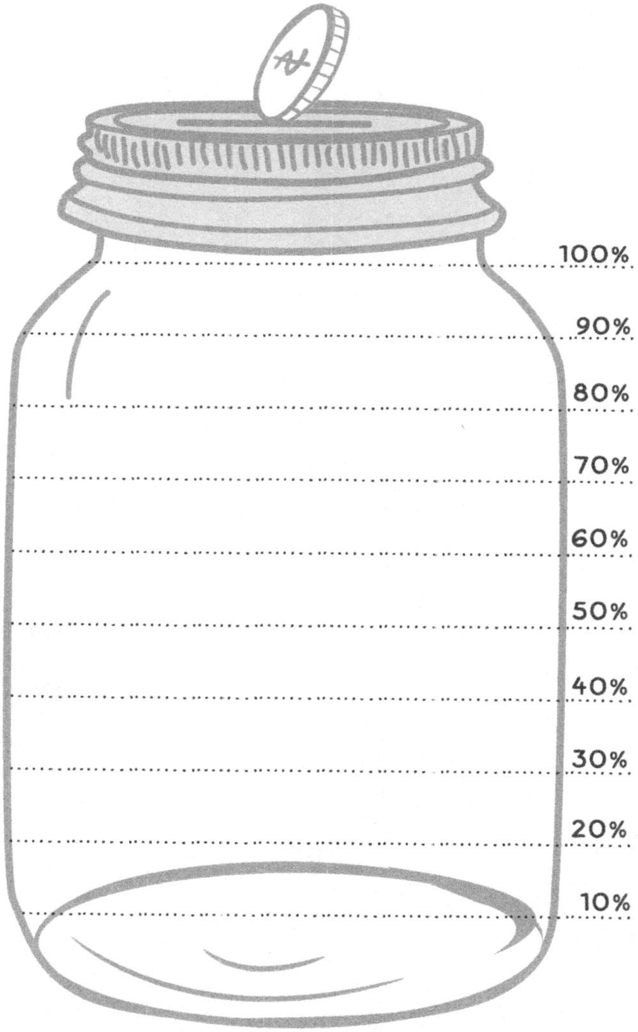

Color in the rows as you save.

Made in the USA
Monee, IL
08 November 2026

67948340R00063